IF YOU'VE GOT IT, HAUNT IT:

50+ WAYS TO PROFIT FROM YOUR OWN HALLOWEEN BUSINESS

by Linda Johnson Tomsho

Cover design and book layout by Bolhuis Design

Cover images © mythja / ShutterStock

Interior images (in order)
Skull - www.thegraphicsfairy.com
Photo of Children in Halloween Costumes © Miss Mustard Seed via www.thegraphicsfairy.com
Bat Lady - www.thegraphicsfairy.com
Cemetery Sketches © kuco /Adobe Stock
Pumpkin Head © kichingin19 /Adobe Stock
Dark Halloween Backdrop - Graphic Stock
Mystic Scene © Slava Gerj /Shutter Stock
Vintage Skull © lynea /Adobe Stock
Vintage Spooky Doll © /Adobe Stock

To my amazing husband, who always has my back and encourages me in everything I do... no matter how weird.

Fig. 4.

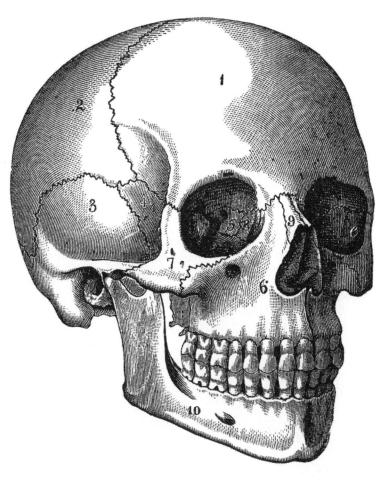

❧ TABLE OF CONTENTS ❧

INTRODUCTION
SO YOU WANT TO BE A HALLOWEEN ENTREPRENEUR?..7

CHAPTER 1
WHAT KIND OF BUSINESS IS RIGHT FOR YOU?......................................13

CHAPTER 2
SELLING A PRODUCT...21

CHAPTER 3
PERFORMING A SERVICE..31

CHAPTER 4
CREATIVE ENDEAVORS...39

CHAPTER 5
ENTERTAINMENT/PERFORMANCE...49

CHAPTER 6
STRICTLY VIRTUAL/YOUR ONLINE BUSINESS......................................55

CHAPTER 7
BRICKS AND MORTAR/YOUR PHYSICAL ASSETS..................................61

PARTING THOUGHTS...67

LINDA JOHNSON TOMSHO (AKA MALEDICTA)......................................69

INTRODUCTION

SO YOU WANT TO BE A
HALLOWEEN ENTREPRENEUR?

In the words of Mick Jagger, "Please allow me to introduce myself…"

I may look like your typical suburban wife and mother of three, movie fanatic, dog rescuer, and entrepreneur, but beneath my conventional exterior, I'm a rabid Halloween enthusiast.

Halloween has always been my favorite holiday of the year… YES, even including Christmas!

I celebrate Halloween in a big way every year with an elaborate party, and I take a lot of pride in decorating my home for the holiday. I seek out unusual decorations and crafts, do research to find the latest in Halloween Technology, and trick out my house and yard. Cars slow down as they pass my house to get a better look at my awesome graveyard and other decorations.

And I don't just celebrate Halloween in October… I lead a "Halloween Lifestyle" all year round. In fact, I've even launched a website – Halloween-Lifestyle.com – to share my love of Halloween with the whole world.

I keep some of my favorite decorations up all year, including a life-size skeleton named Vincent who permanently resides next to the TV. He wears a sombrero for Cinco de Mayo, a Santa hat at Christmas, and 70s sunglasses for Elvis Presley's birthday.

I try to keep the spirit of Halloween alive every month as the hostess and co-founder of a film society dedicated to B-movies and cult films. I'm a life-long devotee of scary movies, and in fact, Godzilla is my favorite movie star.

So what does that have to do with making money from Halloween?

The fact is, there are a lot of other people out there who are just like me.

Perhaps you've heard that Halloween is now the second biggest (and fastest-growing) holiday of the year in terms of consumer spending.

The National Retail Federation predicted that consumer Halloween spending in 2018 would top **$9.1 billion**, with Halloween candy ALONE responsible for **$2.7 billion** in revenue. It was also predicted that pet owners would spend over **$440 million** just on costumes for their fur-kids!

Shouldn't some of that money be in your pocket? Obviously there's plenty of opportunity for a creative entrepreneur to launch a Halloween business and make some money. All it takes is a little ambition, a little imagination, and most importantly – taking those first steps!

I think many people who dream of starting a Halloween business are like me. In fact, if you're reading this, I'm betting you're probably one of my tribe… one of the millions of fellow humans who love Halloween!

But perhaps you're thinking "I really don't care that much about Halloween and all the costumes and decorations and scary stuff. I just want to start a business that will make my bank account happy!"

And that's okay. As long as you recognize the potential profits from doing Halloween-y things and catering to people like me, it doesn't matter if you have a passion for Halloween as long as you have a deep, abiding passion for money. Having fun is just a bonus!

**In other words, you don't have to be a Halloween fanatic
to become a Halloween Entrepreneur, but it helps!**

My mission for this book is to help you find a Halloween business you can love, whether or not you're a Halloween fanatic, and even if you've never started a business before. You'll be surprised how quickly, easily, and cheaply it can be done. And of course, I'll be here to hold your hand and guide you through the process.

Oh yeah? What makes you think you know so much about this stuff?

I wear a lot of hats (and some of them aren't even pointed!).

In addition to being the Founder and CEO (Chief Enthusiasm Officer) of Halloween-Lifestyle.com and the Morbid Emporium, I'm also a Certified Changing Course Career Consultant and Small Business Idea Generator with my career-coaching business, Different Drummer Coaching.

I work with people who want to change their lives, especially the way they earn a living. I love working with people who have "unusual" interests, and I specialize in helping clients who want to start Halloween and Horror-related businesses.

My superpower is "Ideation" – basically, I'm a brainstorming specialist.

My job is to help my clients come up with creative and outside-the-box income-generating ideas that suit their needs, talents, and goals. Then together we figure out how they can earn income from their interests and work at something they enjoy. The ultimate goal is to help my clients launch their own businesses, possibly even escape from their boring jobs, and create a life they can love.

How do I do that? One way is to show them how to develop multiple streams of income based on what they love to do. If they already have a business, I help them create multiple profit centers. And if they have a day job they want to keep, I help them set up a side hustle. It's smart to avoid putting all your financial eggs in one basket! With multiple income streams, you'll always have other profit centers to sustain you if one source dries up.

I do follow my own advice – not only am I a fabulous Internet Maven and Career Consultant, but I also have side hustles as an independent copywriter, a freelance researcher, and book coach.

If you need help with choosing or starting up a business (or multiple business-es), drop me a line at maledicta@Halloween-Lifestyle.com, and I'll hook you up with a free 30-minute Discovery Session.

Size does matter!

You don't have to spend your life savings to start a business (or even multiple businesses). Many of the ideas in this book, not to mention thousands of others that I probably haven't even thought of, can be started on a shoestring.

Obviously we're not talking about what we call a "Big Dream" – a business like a full-blown haunted attraction or a themed restaurant that would require a significant investment – though if you have the means to realize that dream, go for it! For the purposes of this book, I'm mostly focusing on small niche enterprises and boutique businesses, the kind that you can start as a nice little side gig for a minimal investment – sometimes even under $100.

Starting small has the added advantage of allowing you to find out if you like actually doing the business before committing a lot of time and money to it. Let's say you love baking Halloween cookies, but you realize after a while that you really, really hate doing it all day long. If your business is small and agile, when you figure out that it isn't working – maybe it just isn't fun anymore, or it isn't making any money – you can get out before you've invested too much of your resources. And you can congratulate yourself for dodging a bullet!

So what about the rest of the year?

Most Halloween businesses are seasonal, and you'll probably have other irons in the fire. The majority of your income will come between Labor Day and November 1st. But don't forget about the Halloween Lifestyle Tribe – the hundreds of thousands of people out there like me who celebrate Halloween all year.

We are the reason there are permanent bricks-and-mortar Halloween stores (like Halloween Club in Los Angeles or Reinke Brothers in Littleton, Colorado) that stay open 12 months a year, as well as costume stores and online businesses that cater to hardcore Halloween fanatics. There's also a busy convention circuit where, depending on your business, you can sell all year round to your target market of Halloween, fantasy, and horror enthusiasts.

Don't worry about competition

Last but not least, don't get too stressed out if you find that someone else is doing what you wanted to do. That's called validating the market. It confirms that there someone out there is making money doing it, and that there are people out there who want to buy what you're selling. Put your heart into your business, and your uniqueness will set you apart from your competition.

So don't give up if you find out you weren't the first to come up with your idea. Think abundance – there is plenty of business out there, and the world is a very big place. There's enough money for everyone.

Ready to get started? Let's dive in!

CHAPTER 1

WHAT KIND OF BUSINESS IS RIGHT FOR YOU?

If you don't know what you want to do, you're in good company. Most people begin without knowing what kind of business they want to start. All you need to know is that you like the idea of making money from the spooky fun weirdness that is Halloween.

The kind of business you start depends in part on what you have to offer that other people want to buy. It depends on where your interests, your skills, your education or training, and your assets intersect.

If you need some inspiration to choose your business idea, start by examining your own needs and wants as well as your goals.

What are your personal goals for your business? Why do you want to start a Halloween business? How will you integrate it into your life? Or preferably, how does it fit into the life you WANT to have?

Do you want your Halloween business to be a part-time, full-time, or seasonal business? Some entrepreneurs are looking for a seasonal gig with full immersion (40+ hours a week) for the Halloween season, ending in early November. Some want a business they can pursue 12 months a year. And others just want a side gig to bring in cash while they hold down a "real" job or work in their other profit centers.

If you need to keep your day job to pay the bills, that should be your priority. Your Halloween business will be, at least initially, a side gig. Hopefully, there's enough wiggle room in your existing work life to allow you the time and energy to nurture your side business into a full-time moneymaker if that's where your journey takes you.

What are your financial goals? How much income do you hope to bring in? Be realistic! There has to be a match between your idea, what you want or need to earn, and what you want your life to look like.

What is it about Halloween that you find appealing? Do you have an affinity to the horror aspects like zombies, vampires, ghosts, and so on? Or are you more lighthearted in your attitude toward Halloween – more family friendly, perhaps? Would you be more likely to enjoy a scary haunted attraction or something perhaps with less adrenaline involved? If your answer to this question is "Nothing really; I just want to make money," that's okay, too. Just think of it in terms of...

What kind of business suits your personality? This is important if you want to enjoy what you're doing! Are you an introvert or an extrovert or somewhere inbetween? Do you have a flair for the dramatic or do you prefer working behind the scenes? Do you like to work with crowds, small groups, or one-on-one? Or do you prefer to work alone?

What kind of setting do you want work in? Is it indoors or outdoors? In a kitchen or a workshop? A theater or a haunted house?

How do you want to spend your work time? Do you want to spend your time writing? Making videos? Working outdoors? Or would you rather be baking, singing, inventing, or teaching?

The next important question to ask yourself is…

What do you have that other people might want?

More importantly, what do you have that they would PAY FOR? This includes both your physical and intellectual assets, including some you may not even realize you have:

- What training or education do you possess that would benefit your client?
- What are your gifts and talents?
- What hobbies or interests really turn you on? What kinds of books and magazines you like to read? What are your favorite websites?
- What skills do you have that you enjoy using?
- What material assets do you have (or could you get) that you can monetize?

If you're not sure what you have to offer, ask yourself:

- What do people tell you you're really good at?
- What do people ask you for help with?
- What do people compliment you on?

Remember, though something may come easily for you, it may not be so easy for other people, and they will gladly pay you for it.

How can you turn what you have into income?

If you've answered the questions up until now, you have an idea of what kind of business you'd like to start, you know what you love to do and what you're good at. And you know what tangible assets you have that you can monetize.

Now comes the hard part – how do you get people to give you money for those things?

Basically, there are five places to look for income-generating opportunities:

1. Complaints, problems, or threats

What frustrates or annoys people? Example: People who want an impressive yard haunt for Halloween but don't have the time or skills to execute it.

2. Trends

What's hot this year? What coming trends can you get out in front of? Example: Halloween costumes for pets.

3. Niche markets or demographic groups

Example: Halloween cooking class for kids.

4. Interests or hobbies

How can you help other people pursue their own interests? Example: DIY project plans for a Halloween graveyard.

5. Your personal experiences

What experiences in your life can you draw on to teach others or help them? Example: Teach a workshop or webinar on how to run a haunted house.

Who wants what you have?

What kind of person, group, or audience would want what you have to offer? Imagine your ideal client... what do they look like? Are they male or female? Kids, teens, or seniors? What are their interests? This is an important exercise because it helps you to focus your marketing efforts on exactly the people who are most likely to buy.

Beyond your obvious potential clients, whom else could you partner or collaborate with? What group, organization, or other business is trying to attract the same market you are? If your business is photographing pets in their

Halloween costumes, you could partner with a pet store that will let you set up in their space.

Who might sponsor you? It could be an individual, a professional group, an organization, or a company. For example, your local tourism organization could sponsor your tours of a historic local cemetery.

Some other ideas for partnerships:
- Local newspapers and magazines
- Event planners
- Halloween stores
- Health professionals
- Candy stores
- Costume rental stores
- Historical societies
- Adult education programs
- Advocacy groups
- Websites that share your interests,

What are the first steps you need to take to start your business?

You'd be surprised how many people want to start a business but never pursue their dream simply because they don't know what to do first.

Actually, that first step is simple: **Find the information and resources you need to move forward.**

So how do you do that? First, ask for advice from someone who's done it already. Contact other business owners (or artists or performers or writers) in your market – they're your best source of information about how to get into the business and what it's really like. Advice from fellow business owners is extremely valuable for a newbie... so in other words, JUST ASK!

Just a polite phone call or email is all that's needed. You may be pleasantly surprised at their willingness to give advice to someone who's just getting into the business. Of course, some may see you as a potential competitor and treat you with suspicion, so don't be discouraged if not everyone is helpful.

Do your research!

It's amazing how much information you can ferret out just by doing a smart Google search. There are plentiful online resources available about how to do just about any kind of business. While you're doing your research, don't forget to find out what other similar businesses are doing – especially **what they are doing well**. How are they attracting clients? How do they adjust to market changes? How could you emulate them?

While you have your researcher hat on, find out what other businesses similar to yours are charging for their products and services. If that business isn't in the same geographical area, adjust your expectations based on your local economy.

Prepare to Launch: Next Steps

Find resources for free or low-cost business advice in your local area. Google "small business help" or "small business advice" to find the local offices for organizations like SCORE and the Small Business Administration. Also search for Small Business Development Centers (SBDC) in your community, another excellent resource for entrepreneurial mentoring and learning opportunities.

Hang out with other entrepreneurs. Network, network, network!

Learn some basic marketing techniques. How email marketing works, writing a sales page, social media… whatever is needed for your unique business.

Get a handle on the money aspects of starting up, like how much money do you need to launch? How much should you charge? How much can you expect to make from this business?

Do you need to write a business plan? In my opinion, probably not. Unless you're trying to obtain outside funding, a traditional business plan is overkill. Mike Michalowicz lays out an alternative "Prosperity Plan" in his cult-classic book *The Toilet Paper Entrepreneur*, which I highly recommend. Your plan, which can just be a page or two, should simply consist of what you want to do and why, your end goals for the business, how you will do it, and who you will do it with and for.

Keep a journal. It helps you remember things and keep your thoughts organized.

And my #1 best piece of advice for a successful launch is… Do something that moves your business forward EVERY DAY. No matter how small, just do something!

So now that you have an idea of where to start, where do you go from here?

Depending on your own skill set, talents, and assets, there are five different types of businesses you might consider:

- Selling a Product
- Providing a Service
- Creative Pursuits
- Entertainment and Performance
- Tangible Assets (a building, a vehicle, etc.)

We'll explore each these options in the coming chapters. There will obviously be some overlap in the categories, and some businesses will cross over more than one category. You should always be thinking – "What do I have that other people will pay for?"

This is hardly a definitive list of every possible Halloween business out there. I've tried to give you a lot of ideas to inspire you, but with a little imagination, I'm sure you can come up with many more!

CHAPTER 2

SELLING A PRODUCT

One of the best ways to make money from Halloween mania is to sell a product. People tend to have their wallets out already, and Halloween fanatics are always looking for something new, exciting, and unique to spend their money on.

If you decide that a product-based business is the way you want to go, you have some decisions to make:

First, do you want to sell a product that you make yourself? Or do you want to sell a product that is made by someone else (in other words, you're a reseller)?

What kind of product do you want to sell? A tangible physical product? Or a virtual product like an EBook or other information product?

How do you want to sell your product?

- Sell from your own website.
- Sell through a bricks-and-mortar store.
- Sell at events.
- Sell for someone else as an affiliate.
- Affiliates sell your product for you.
- Sell through a third-party entity like Craigslist, Amazon, or Etsy.

Depending on the product, you can sell via one of these venues or possibly all of them, as some products lend themselves to multiple marketing techniques.

Top Ten ideas for a product-based Halloween business

1. Selling costumes and accessories

Or more specifically, buying and reselling costumes and accessories. This is part of my **#1 Best Halloween Moneymaking Strategy,** and I'm going to share it with you right now:

> *Buy as many leftover Halloween costumes and accessories (wigs, jewelry, fake weapons, you name it) as you possibly can when these items go on clearance the day after Halloween, then resell them for a profit the following year.*

This strategy does require some investment and some patience because it won't pay off until next fall, but if you're smart and make good choices, you can make some serious cash.

As you probably know, seasonal Halloween stores like Spirit Halloween and Halloween Express typically set up shop in a vacant storefront in early September and sell a ton of Halloween merchandise between then and October 31st. But on November 1st, they slash their prices 50% or more to clear out the merchandise. A few days later, they close up and ship out all the remaining stock to a warehouse to await next year's Halloween season.

But here's where YOU come in – and clean up! Just show up early on November 1st and buy that merchandise at rock bottom prices. Bring a lot of cash and/or make sure your credit cards have plenty of room available – you are investing in your inventory for next year. Granted, you have to be patient, and you must have a clean, dry place to store your booty for 10 months. But when September arrives, you'll be able to reap a tidy profit.

A word of advice… always stick with the classics: Vampires, ghosts, witches, devils, zombies, and the like. Classic superheroes like Superman and Batman are also a good bet. Presidential masks (only of the current president, though Nixon is a favorite year after year!) are also perennial bestsellers.

However, don't invest in any other costumes that are topical – that is, they're related to currently popular TV or movie characters or something that is a current fad. People will forget about the movie, or the show may be canceled, and then next year, it won't be a thing anymore. It won't sell, and you'll be stuck with it.

Just think of all those Jersey Shore costumes languishing in warehouses somewhere… Back in 1987, TV character Max Headroom was one of the top-selling costumes. Then the show was canceled, and he was forgotten by the following Halloween season. Of course, if you can hang onto the costume for about 30 years, you can make a fortune selling rare nostalgia!

Which brings me to my #2 Best Halloween Moneymaking Strategy:

In your search for big day-after-Halloween clearance sales, don't overlook grocery stores, department stores, and dollar stores as sources for your inventory! They often have even better markdowns than the Halloween stores.

If you want to sell costumes and accessories that you make or modify yourself, I have one more secret to share!

My #3 Best Halloween Moneymaking Strategy:
The thrift shop is your best friend!

Unlike Clearance Chasing, which lasts for only a few days after Halloween, you can be scouting thrift shops all year round for costumes or costume components. I suggest you "haunt" shops in more upscale neighborhoods, as they generally have better quality merchandise and more selection. Use your imagination and come prepared with ideas for costumes, but also be open to inspiration while you shop. I've purchased overalls, fur wraps, military uniforms, tons of costume jewelry, boots, shawls, hats, and all kinds of other things and repurposed them into my own costume creations.

What kinds of costumes can you make from thrift store finds? Here are some that I've assembled through a combination of post-Halloween clearance and thrifting expeditions:

- Trailer Park Housewife: Housecoat, hairnet, curlers, fuzzy slippers, hairnet, copy of the National Enquirer, and Catwoman glasses
- Serial Killer: Mechanic's jumpsuit, hockey mask, and plastic knife
- Indiana Jones: Khakis, leather jacket, white button down shirt, explorer hat, and whip

Another option is to take those clearance costumes or thrift shop treasures, refurbish or improve them with your sewing or crafting skills, and then sell or rent your customized creations. (More about moneymaking ideas for crafty/creative people in Chapter 4.)

2. Halloween decorations and props

My #1 Best Halloween Moneymaking Strategy also works for Halloween decorations and props. Like costumes, they can also be acquired at rock-bottom prices at temporary Halloween stores, grocery stores, drug stores, dollar stores, and department stores during the short window immediately after Halloween. And don't forget that the thrift store is a great source for components to make your own creations.

A savvy entrepreneur who wants to resell decorations and props should carefully keep tabs on any new developments in Halloween Technology. The reason for this is because only the people who are really into Halloween will be on top of these technological advances. They tend to be very competitive and will buy them and incorporate them into their displays as soon as they hit the market. Those Early Adopters will be the first to display them, and then the neighbors will see them and go mad with envy. As a result, there will be a much greater demand for those items the following year.

What should you look for? Again, anything new and different on the market may be a hot seller next year. Some items are evergreen (meaning they sell well year after year), including faux tombstones, lights, cobwebs and netting, life-size skeletons, cauldrons, etc. And again, as with costumes and Halloween gear, avoid trendy items based on current fads or popular TV shows or movies that will probably be forgotten by next September.

3. Halloween-themed wearables

No doubt you've seen them around in the month of October; T-shirts, hats, hoodies, and more bearing a Halloween message. And for those of us who are Halloween Lifestyle enthusiasts, gothic or horror-themed apparel is something we may wear at any time of the year!

You can create and sell your own Halloween-themed garments without much in the way of design skills, but if you're fluent in Photoshop or Paint Shop Pro, you have a lot more flexibility. Just come up with suitable Halloweenish words or graphics, and one-stop shops like Café Press or Spreadshirt will print whatever you want on your garments. You can also get your designs reproduced on mugs, tote bags, and other accessories.

4. Vintage Halloween collectibles

Because there are so many of us who are into the holiday, Halloween collectibles are a big seller all year round. The strategy is to keep a lookout at local yard sales, thrift shops, , antique stores, and flea markets and frequent sites like EBay, Amazon, and Craigslist for vintage Halloween items, including:

Costumes	Masks	Board Games
Sheet Music	Postcards	Lanterns
Decorations	Magazines	Books
Diecuts	Candy Containers	

You can sell your treasures from your own website or resell them directly through Etsy, EBay, Amazon, or Craigslist. Also, websites like VintageHalloween.org (where Halloween fans are likely to hang out) provide a marketplace where sellers can post their stuff for sale.

5. Custom treat bags for kids

Some people are super busy, and though their hearts are in the right place, they don't have the time to prepare for the annual trick-or-treat ritual. Or maybe they're hosting a Halloween party for kids. Others may be opposed to distributing candy due to nutritional concerns. You can make them all look like heroes when they hand out your custom treat bags on Halloween night or at a Halloween party.

In addition to the individuals mentioned above, potential customers for this product could be elementary school teachers, Sunday schools, Scouts, PTAs, neighborhood associations, or any organization that sponsors Halloween festivities for kids.

Start by collecting small toys, pencils, stickers, temporary tattoos, etc., and package them in cute Halloween-themed bags. Again, you can also get super deals on these items on clearance at grocery stores, dollar stores, and department stores after the holiday and save them for next year. They can also be bought very inexpensively and in bulk from online stores like www.oriental-trading.com. You can even get the bags from there, or make them yourself with small paper bags decorated with orange and black Halloween stamps and tied with orange and black ribbon. Do check to make sure the items you want to include in the bags are appropriate for the ages of the children who will receive them – i.e., you don't want to give small items to children under 3.

If you want to include candy, you can buy it in large bags at a warehouse club store (Costco or Sam's Club), and check for good deals online. Needless to say, candy is not one of those things you should buy now to save for next year.

6 "Treat bags" for businesses

Local service businesses on the idea of treat bags for their customers. Depending on what your client wants each bag can contain candy, a brochure, an advertising specialty tem (like a keychain, pen, or other item with the company's name or logo on it), and a coupon or certificate for a special offer. As described above, preprinted bags with Halloween themes are available from various places online and offline, or if you're crafty, you can make your own.

7 Homemade Halloween sweets

Put your baking or candy-making skills to work producing homemade Halloween-themed cookies, cupcakes, or candy. You can take pre-orders for delivery at a scheduled date, or you can get a table at a farmer's market, fall festival, or craft fair to sell directly to the public. Check first to see if any permits or licenses are needed to sell food products in your local area.

8 Halloween Cookbook

If you want to make it an EBook, this one is pretty easy and can be turned around in no time. Just collect your favorite ghoulish recipes and format them into a book for Kindle or another self-publishing site. You can also format your book as a pdf and sell it on your own website or through affiliate sites (see #10). And if you want to go full-on Old School, get it printed. You can sell at local venues or seasonal markets. Ask local bookstores and shops if they would be willing to sell it on consignment.

9 Information Products

This broad category includes anything that gets your knowledge out of your head and in front of other people to make you money. You can take your own Halloween expertise or the expertise of others and organize it, package it, and make a profit on it. Even if the information is easily found on the internet, most people won't take the time and effort required to do their own research, and you can profit by collecting it in one place for them.

Information products can be printed books, EBooks, tip sheets, how-to guides, podcasts, and more. Chapter 6 will go into more detail about information products.

10. Affiliate Sales

If marketing isn't your thing, there's still a way for you to sell your product online. Instead of doing it yourself, you can enlist affiliates online who will promote your products to their own mailing lists or advertise them for you in exchange for a cut of your sales.

Online affiliate sales of Halloween-related items has great potential for significant profit. There are dozens if not hundreds of reputable affiliate programs online that pay out generous commissions. A couple examples are Clickbank. com and cj.com. Just Google your particular area of interest to find the best fit for you. Of course, you can also design your own affiliate program and recruit affiliates on your own.

CHAPTER 3

PERFORMING A SERVICE

For several reasons, a service-based business may be your fastest and easiest path to cash in on the Halloween season. Often a service business can be launched on a shoestring, requires little or no inventory, and in many cases, all you have to do is hang out a shingle and start marketing.

A service business is a natural choice for the 21st century entrepreneur. We all lead incredibly busy lives. And we often feel there aren't enough hours in the day to finish everything on our To-Do lists! We're happy to pay someone to do the heavy lifting for us.

Some people love Halloween and want to celebrate in a big way, but the demands of work, parenthood, and other necessary things get in the way. Many of them are willing to spend money on Halloween fun and impressing their friends and neighbors, but they just don't have enough TIME... there's not enough time to do the research to decide what they want... not enough time to find the resources to do it... and not enough time to create what they want. Or maybe they have the time, but they don't have the artistic talent or the building skills to do it themselves. **These people are your potential clients!**

Here's where you come in! By offering your service, you're helping your customer have a happy Halloween when they lack the time or skills to create it for themselves.

Thinking back to Chapter 1, what skills or experience do you have that you could put to work for clients in a service-based Halloween business?

Top Ten ideas for a service-based Halloween businesses

1. Halloween Party Planning

Do you have a reputation for throwing awesome parties? Put your skills to work planning Halloween parties for others. With great atmosphere, music, food, and drinks, your clients will be the envy of their social circle.

You can provide general party planning services, or you can specialize in parties for a particular age group or demographic (teens, singles, etc.). Also, you can offer your services to plan/run a party for a private host or for an organization like a neighborhood group, a church, an apartment complex, a bar, etc.

Details of the planning process, selecting food and décor, and so on, depend on the age group of the attendees. Kids prefer simple foods and treats that can be eaten on the go. They like age-appropriate spooky stuff (but not TOO scary!), games, and prizes. Kids' parties usually last just a couple hours.

A party for adults would be more likely to probably involve more scary-type décor, different activities, and more adult food and beverage choices.

Sometimes shopping centers or neighborhood associations will sponsor entertainment as a trick-or-treat alternative on Halloween night to keep kids safely off the streets. Church groups may also throw parties for children for safety reasons or to de-emphasize the occult aspect of the holiday.

Where do you get cool ideas for your clients' parties? There are plenty of excellent books and websites with fabulous Halloween ideas. Martha Stewart. com is my favorite source for decorating ideas and well as delicious recipes.

Here's another example of cashing in on a trend – smart entrepreneurs are making a ton of money by creating customized candy buffets for Halloween parties. Start by acquiring a few folding tables with table linens in Halloween colors and appropriately spooky decorations. Remember **my #3 Best Halloween Moneymaking Strategy from Chapter 2?** The thrift shop is your friend because it's a great place to find all sorts of glass jars (also brandy snifters, trifle bowls, or any other clear container) for very little investment to display the candy. Again, you can buy the candy itself through bulk sources online or at local warehouse stores.

2. Halloween Party DJ

Either as an added bonus to your party-planning service or as an independent service, if you have the equipment and the know-how, you can offer your expertise as a DJ and/or MC for the party to keep things lively and running smoothly. It's a good fit for just about any kind of Halloween party. Of course, you should plan your musical program based on the age group and preferences of your partygoers.

3. Decorating Businesses or Homes

Another example of a client who wants a fabulous holiday display but lacks the time, inspiration, or energy to do it themselves. There are people out there with plenty of money and the desire to impress with an awesome haunted yard scenario, and they'll be happy to pay you to make it happen instead of having to do the planning, shopping, set-up, and takedown themselves.

You can provide your own décor that you scoop up when it goes on clearance the previous year (again, see **My #1 Best Halloween Moneymaking Strategy** in Chapter 2). Or you can purchase the specific décor that your client wants and add it to your invoice.

4. Pumpkin Carving

Do you have a talent for creating scary/funny/artistic jack-o-lanterns? You can create amazingly detailed pumpkins with simple tools you can buy in a grocery store or online. As you become more skilled, you can invest in a set of lino cutting tools (used for printmaking), drills, and clay sculpting tools.

Research potential designs on the internet – there are plenty of great sites with free or inexpensive designs. My personal favorite is www.zombiepumpkins. com. You can show clients the designs you can make online, or you can carve them into pumpkins ahead of the season and photograph them for your website or catalog. Or create a permanent demo from one of those foam artificial pumpkins sold at craft stores.

One more great thing about this business, it generates its own secondary income stream – selling the leftover pumpkin seeds! You can even offer multiple flavor options like teriyaki, curry, cinnamon spice, and Cajun.

5. Applying Halloween Makeup

If you're skilled at applying special effects makeup, you can make a ton of cash during the Halloween season. You may already have a professional makeup kit if you're a pro or serious hobbyist. If not, you can get started with a basic makeup kit from a Halloween store or online. You can book gigs for parties (children or adults), or you can reserve a table at a farmer's market, craft fair, or Halloween event. Do some practice jobs and photograph them to build a portfolio of your work to show potential customers.

6. Haunted Attraction Tours

So you may not have the resources, manpower, and skill to create a haunted attraction of your own… but you definitely could transport a group to someone else's attraction.

Purchase tickets in bulk or negotiate a group rate from the attractions you plan to visit. Rent a van or a limo, depending on how fancy you want it to be (make sure you have the proper insurance!), and take reservations for a tour of local haunted houses. It's an attractive option for people who would rather someone else did the driving. You can even offer snacks and drinks to your passengers. To maximize your potential profits, you can also recruit sponsors to fill swag bags with their advertising materials, candy, coupons, and so on.

Alternatively, you can put together your own tours, like ghost tours or murder or scandal tours in your local area. More detail on that in Chapter 5.

7. Costume Rental and Alterations

Time to deploy those costumes and accessories you bought on clearance (remember **My #1 Best Halloween Moneymaking Strategy** from Chapter 2?). But instead of selling them, you can rent them out to partygoers. Entrepreneur Cheryl Harmon did just that when she started her costume rental business in Indianapolis, where she uses her sewing skills to repurpose costumes and thrift store finds into one-of-a-kind creations.

High-quality theatrical costumes will not only command a higher price, but they'll also hold up longer because they're better made. Rent them overnight or for a three-day period, and collect your fee up front! Since your business would mostly be local, you can distribute flyers or advertise on Craigslist or in local papers. One local business in my area sets up a tent at the local Renaissance Festival every year, renting costumes for the day for visitors who really want to get into the Renaissance spirit!

8. Trick-or-Treat Services

Halloween night can present logistical problems for busy families. You can provide an easy solution! Here are a few ways you can make a few extra bucks by helping out on Halloween night:

Halloween Photographer/Videographer: Create happy Halloween memories by taking professional pictures and/or video of the kids in their costumes. You can also shoot video of the kids making their trick-or-treat rounds of the neighborhood.

Childcare: If you have a way with kids, you can offer childcare services while the parents go off to celebrate at an adult party. You can make things festive for the kids with a little party of their own, and by accepting multiple children (with help if necessary) you can multiply your profits.

Petsitting: Family dogs can present a problem on Halloween night because they may bark or become aggressive with masked strangers knocking at the door. You can provide a special Halloween petsitting service (with pickup and dropoff) to keep them out of trouble. Better yet, why not put on a Halloween party for dogs? They like treat bags, too!

Trick-or-Treat Escort: You can escort the kids around the neighborhood for trick-or-treat or take them to a community event.

9. Teach your skills to others

Create a workshop where you teach attendees how to do something you do well. A lot of people would love to learn how to carve an intricate pumpkin, apply makeup, or build Halloween props. You can also create a workshop on horror fiction writing, party planning, or maybe even… how to start a Halloween business!

10. Work at someone else's Halloween business

If you're not looking to start your own business and just want to earn some extra cash, consider taking a seasonal job in the Halloween industry:

Work at a pumpkin patch driving the tractor for the hayride wagon, selling cider and funnel cakes, or manning a cash register.

Get a seasonal job at a pop-up Halloween store like Spirit Halloween or Halloween Express. Google the stores by name, and you'll find online employment applications. They generally pay minimum wage or a little better, but it's a fun way to bring in extra money while indulging your love of Halloween at the same time. The season ends a few days after Halloween, but some stores go on to sell Christmas merchandise in the same space, so you might be able to stretch out the gig until the first of the year.

Theme parks hire a lot of seasonal employees for their Halloween festivities. Depending on your skills, you can help build the temporary haunted attractions, you can help wire them for light and sound, or you can be a performer – a zombie, vampire, serial killer, etc.

They also need cashiers, food vendors, and ride operators just like any other time of year. You can just take tickets or sell hot chocolate and enjoy the Halloween spirit!

One advantage to working Halloween at a theme park – it allows you plenty of time during the day to work at another job or on your own projects.

CHAPTER 4

CREATIVE ENDEAVORS

Creative people are really in their element during the Halloween season! If you're artistic, have a way with words, if you're crafty or musical, or if you know your way around a stage, there are plenty of ways to make money with a Halloween business.

There's a bit of overlap between this chapter and product or service businesses described in Chapter 2 or Chapter 3. This chapter, however, specifically deals with businesses where you're selling something that is a direct product of your creativity.

I could easily devote an entire book to creative Halloween things you can do to make money (maybe a book for next year?). Some have a market that buys all year round and can generate income not just in the fall, but in spring, summer, and winter as well. Remember, there are a lot of people like me out there!

30+ Ways to Turn Your Creativity into Halloween Cash

If you're a writer...

Your talent for writing can bring in a lot of cash during the Halloween season. It's also a skill that you can put to use creating content for Halloween fiends and other assorted lovers of the macabre all year round!

Here are some suggestions for Halloween-themed writing projects:

Write a book: Collect your stash of Halloween tips, recipes, or how-to instructions, and put them into book form. Your book can be a resource for practical information. Or if you're more the literary type, perhaps you could put together a collection of poetry or stories with illustrations (either your own or works that are in the public domain).

Of course, EBooks are far easier to produce than print books, and it's never been easier to put together a book and sell it online. You can sell your book online from your own website (or create a single sales page just for your book), or you can upload it to Kindle or another web publisher.

Kindle is a great format and very flexible for writing and promoting your book the way you want it. There are plenty of online guides to self-publishing on the internet; just Google until you find what you need. More details about publishing online in Chapter 6.

Create a Halloween website: Are you fluent in HTML? A Halloween website could become a lucrative business for you! Your site can be big or small, depending on how much content you have to offer. As long as the site is easy to navigate with colorful images, you can decide what sort of content would appeal to your target audience.

The site can feature your blog or articles, stories, Halloween-centered art, and reviews of films, books, haunted houses, and new technology, just to throw out a few ideas. Another option is to maintain an aggregator site. This is a site that offers "one-stop shopping" for Halloween information by collecting and organizing online and offline resources for Halloween lovers. Your readers can click through to other sites where they can find stuff they need.

Monetize your site by selling banner ads or classifieds and by charging other websites to be listed in your directories. A very profitable alternative is to join other sites' affiliate programs where you run their ads on your site, then when one of your page visitors clicks through and buys their product, you get a percentage of the sale.

Visit my website, Halloween-Lifestyle.com, to see some of these concepts in action.

Write DIY guides for Halloween prop making: If you're a skilled prop builder, you can sell plans, materials lists, and instructions for unique props like floating ghosts, eerie graveyards, and scenes from the zombie apocalypse. You can sell them from your own website, advertise, or become an affiliate on other sites that specialize in Halloween do-it-yourself projects. Because the guides would be relatively short in length, you might also consider printing them out and selling them locally.

Write articles about haunted destinations or spooky subjects: Halloween-related topics are of interest to the right publications and websites for their October issues. However, if you want to sell to a magazine, you need to plan, query, and write the articles well in advance – sometimes nearly a year before the issue goes to press. In other words, you could be offering your Halloween décor article to an editor in January. Always check the editorial calendar of any publication where you want to submit your work.

Submitting articles to online publications can be accomplished by email and doesn't require nearly as much lead time. Again, inquire far in advance about deadlines for their Halloween issues.

There are also magazines and websites out there that publish year-round for horror fans and Halloween Lifestyle folks. They offer a perennial audience for articles on the haunted attraction trade, do-it-yourself propbuilding and costuming, effects creation, and horror fiction, to name a few. As always, Google is your friend!

Are you an expert at photography or video?

You can put your camera skills (digital, film, or video) to work with one or more of these ideas to generate Halloween income:

Sell your photos of Halloween-themed subjects to stock photo companies, who are always eager for unusual or novelty photos to sell their customers. They'll pay you for the photograph, plus you'll receive a small commission anytime someone downloads your work.

Scan or download vintage photographs and modify them with Adobe Photoshop to turn them into spooky Halloween-type pictures, then sell them on your website.

Create Halloween cards or notecards: With that same idea, you can create Halloween cards or notecards with your own photos and designs. Again, you can sell them online on your own or someone else's website, or you can ask local merchants to sell them on consignment.

Take Halloween portraits of kids or pets in costume: How about Halloween family portraits with backdrops and props... perhaps an Addams Family motif? You come to the home, or you can set up your "studio" in a central location.

Photo service at conventions: Many of the Halloween or horror-oriented "cons" sell vendor space to photographers. A lot of people (they're called cosplayers) like to attend these events dressed up in costumes modeled after characters in movies, animation, or comics. Your portable studio offers them a way to remember how great they looked with a professional portrait.

Start a Photo Booth Business: There's money to be made at Halloween parties with a photo booth business! You don't have to be a skilled photographer to succeed with a photo booth – just knowing the basic settings that you'll use at events is enough. Once you've figured that out, the rest is just keeping an eye on the booth and keeping it stocked with photo paper. The booths are most commonly seen at weddings, but any party is potential business… and a Halloween party is an event where people want to remember what they and their friends looked like!

It's easiest to get into the photo booth business by watching classified ads for someone who's looking to get OUT of the business. The initial investment may be greater, but the potential is there to make full-time money from a weekend side hustle.

Are you an artist or graphic designer?

There's an evergreen market for original art based on Halloween or general macabre themes. If you can create original works of art in this genre, you'll have no trouble selling it during the Halloween season and beyond.

Sell your art on the convention circuit: Conferences that cater to Geek Culture audiences (ComiCon, DragonCon, Steel City Con, etc.) are the perfect places to find buyers for your work.

Create your own line of Halloween cards with your own designs: In addition to greeting cards, you can make notecards, postcards, and calling cards. The same designs could also look great on notebook covers or posters.

Halloween wearables featuring your own designs: See Halloween Wearables in Chapter 2.

Creepy caricatures: Set up your easel at a farmer's market, festival, or Halloween party and draw caricatures of guests as classic monsters —werewolf, vampire, witch, etc. You could also do this business online working from photographs.

Business-to-Business: Small businesses need Halloween-themed advertising at this time of year. You can design postcards, print ads, posters, brochures, and online campaigns for their Halloween promotions.

Are you a "crafty" individual?

More and more people are getting into cool craft projects for Halloween. Many of us like the creative outlet and do it ourselves. But there are also a lot of people who want the finished product but don't have the time or talent to undertake the project themselves.

The internet is full of free information and project plans for Halloween crafters. (Thanks, Internet!) Here are some examples of craft items that you can make and sell for profit:

- Themed wreaths, silk flower arrangements, and centerpieces
- Candles or luminaria
- Window silhouettes
- Halloween trees
- Halloween village miniatures
- Faux tombstones
- Halloween-themed ceramics
- Haunted gingerbread houses (why should they just be for Christmas?)

Are you a whiz with a sewing machine?

In earlier chapters, I talked about modifying thrift shop and clearance finds to sell as a product or to run a costume rental business. Here are a few more moneymaking ideas for people who love to sew:

Creating custom costumes: Though most people wear costumes for Halloween, lots of people buy them for other occasions throughout the year. Halloween may be the busiest season for costume makers, but you can sell custom tailored costumes all year round to people who participate in:

- Renaissance Festivals
- Historical reenactments – Civil War, living history sites, etc.
- Cosplay (performance art involving costumes based on a character in a film, animation, comic, or video game)
- Theater companies

Sew costumes for pets: In 2017, 16% of American pet owners dressed their pets in Halloween costumes. Options at the pet store are limited, especially if you have a large dog, so there's a wide-open market for unusual and creative pet costumes. And why not create your own niche and design costumes for less conventional pets like guinea pigs, parrots, or iguanas?

You can also resell pet costumes that you purchased the previous year on clearance and possibly even tailor them to provide a perfect fit for the lucky pets who get to wear them.

Make patterns for people to sew their own costumes for humans or pets. Some people might want to do it themselves but don't know how.

Sew Halloween flags and banners: Colorful flags and banners of your own design will look great flying from a porch, balcony, or flagpole.

Do you know how to make awesome props?

If they love Halloween, people who are good at mechanical stuff and building things often make money by creating and selling impressive original Halloween props. You can either make props based on someone else's plans, or you can design them from scratch yourself. Plans for cool and spooky indoor and outdoor props like graveyards, strobe-lit ghostly figures, and creaking coffins are widely available on the internet at little or no cost.

Sell DIY instructions: In addition to building and selling unique indoor and outdoor props, if it's one of your own creations, you can also write up step-by-step directions and sell them to DIY enthusiasts.

Use your sculpting skills: They can really come in handy for creating realistic-looking, life-like creatures, tombstones, and unique décor items. Jim Brown of Evansville, Indiana, started his own prop business, Eville J's Creepy Closet, after creating gruesome Halloween sculpture props in his garage for 15 years.

Create and sell monster masks: Eville J's also makes custom masks, molded and painted, for perfectionist Halloween maniacs. A Halloween store mask just isn't good enough!

Make your own custom tombstones: Graveyards are one of most popular outdoor haunts, and creating custom tombstones from wood, foam, concrete, and wire could be a fun way to make some cash during the Halloween season.

If you're a special effects/Halloween makeup artist...

See Chapter 3. You can also make your own video tutorials demonstrating specific makeup techniques and effects.

Do you love to make jewelry?

Just take a look around – jewelry with Goth themes, skulls, spiders, and such is all the rage, and not just at Halloween! Though your business may make the most money during the Halloween season, this is definitely a business that is easily sustainable all year. Sell through your own website, on Etsy, or have others sell for you as affiliates or on consignment. Check your local event calendars for events such as a Maker Faire or a market for crafters such as Pittsburgh's Handmade Arcade.

Do you love to cook or bake?

This was covered in part in Chapter 2. Here are some other ways you can generate cash for Halloween with your culinary skills:

Offer your services as a personal chef for an atmospheric/romantic Halloween dinner for two.

Cater a Halloween party: Create an awesome buffet with thematically appropriate foods like radioactive glowing green punch, dips served from skulls... you get the idea!

Bake Halloween cakes, cookies, or pies: See Chapter 2.

Make gourmet Halloween candy for adults: Maybe something like liqueur-infused decorated truffles or maybe jalapeno candy corn?

Create a custom tea blend for Halloween: You can sell it online or locally.

Do you have music/sound editing skills?

You don't have to be a musician to make money with music! There's plenty of opportunity for someone who's fluent with music and sound technology to generate Halloween cash. (Music Performance will be covered in Chapter 5.)

Create a recording of eerie atmospheric music and/or sound effects and make it available for online download or distribute it on MP3s. Perfect for a Halloween party, or for a YouTube video, or you can sell it to a haunted attraction for ambient music. Some websites offer royalty-free sound files that you can buy and download.

If you're an experienced DJ or MC, you can provide the soundtrack/narration for a Halloween party.

And no matter what your creative talent is...

You can always teach others how to do what you do through live workshops or webinars or producing online video tutorials.

CHAPTER 5

ENTERTAINMENT/PERFORMANCE

If you're a natural-born performer, Halloween could be your happiest time of the year! Depending on your talents, you can stage your own show, perform in someone else's show, or create a product of your own that you can sell again and again.

Top Ten ideas for a Halloween Entertainment business

1. Perform magic

If you're adept at sleight-of-hand and illusions, there's always a market for magic. To make money from your magic skills, you can either do a magic show for a school group, community organization, Scouts, or party, or you can book gigs where you'll perform walk-around magic instead of a stage show.

2. Organize an old-fashioned Spook Show

If you haven't heard of Spook Shows, it's probably because you're too young! The Spook Show is a fun tradition that seems to be making a comeback.

Back in the old days, they would put together shows with magic, comedy, some spooky effects, a cartoon or two, and a scary movie to entertain kids or adults at Halloween. The shows would take place at neighborhood theaters and school auditoriums. Despite the wonderful lurid posters promising ghosts, walking skeletons, and monsters in the theater, the shows are more campy than scary, and it's all in fun

3. The Rocky Horror Picture Show

If I have to tell you what it's about, it probably isn't for you. But if you're a Rocky fan, you can take a party to a midnight showing, book your own screening and organize an event around it, or perhaps have a Rocky Horror-themed costume party with dance-offs and prizes for Best Costume and Best Performance.

4. Read scary stories and record them

Do you have a voice that's perfect for reading tales of terror? Record yourself reading Edgar Allan Poe or HP Lovecraft stories and sell it on an MP3. If you're good with audio, you can even add your own sound effects like thunder, howling wolves, and eerie music.

5. Costumed Character for Hire

Get a high-quality costume (scary clown, vampire, zombie) and rent yourself out to add flavor to other people's Halloween events. Or you can follow the example of evilclownforhire.com, where clients pay to have the person of their choice stalked by Stalky the Evil Clown (in a nonthreatening way, of course!).

If killer clowns aren't your cup of tea, maybe you're more the literary type. You can still go with the costumed character motif and create a living history show; essentially, you dress up as a historical literary figure like Edgar Allan Poe or Mary Shelley and give a talk, performing in character.

6. Organize a Halloween film festival

Use your own venue if you have one, or rent a location. You can book the films (there will be a licensing fee), sell popcorn and snacks, and decorate on your own, but if you don't want to do all the work yourself, there are small businesses that will set up a movie theater (outdoor or indoor) at your location. They take care of any licensing issues and can handle seating, lighting, and food and beverage service.

7. Make a recording of your eerie music

Perform haunting music and sell it as an MP3 online.

8. Busking

Busking, or performing on the street for tips, is a quick and easy way to generate some cash if you're a singer, musician, or magician.

9. Book yourself as a solo musical act or as part of a band or ensemble

Halloween-themed acts can perform at parties, theme park Halloween Nights, or fall festivals.

10 Work as an actor at a haunted attraction

Haunting is a fun and unique job for those who enjoy scaring the snot out of other people! Some haunted houses are more theatrical and want you to do real acting like reciting monologues. Others just want you to jump out and scare people. Some haunts are strictly PG, and others are R-rated and border-line crazy. Figure out where they are on that spectrum and choose the haunt that would be the best fit for you, based on what you like and what you're comfortable with.

Some of them will assign you a character, but some may be open to you portraying a character you've developed on your own.

A beginning actor is most likely to get hired by a community or charity haunt.

If you're interested in working as an actor at a haunted attraction, check out their website. Get their contact information and send them an email, pick up the phone, friend them on Facebook – introduce your self and ask about working for them as an actor.

Theme parks also often have Halloween events for the month of October and need actors to play serial killers, monsters, zombies, vampires, and so on. They also hire performers to keep customers from growing restless while standing in long lines. For example, magician/mentalist Alexander Vornoff (in costume as an evil pirate) has entertained guests with walk-around magic as they waited in line to enter a haunted house attraction at Kennywood Park's Phantom Fright Nights.

In fact, some haunted attractions are open all year round. So if you love Halloween so much that you're open to an ongoing gig, you can look for long-term employment

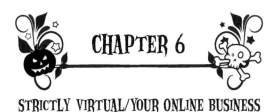

CHAPTER 6

STRICTLY VIRTUAL/YOUR ONLINE BUSINESS

This chapter is devoted to businesses that are done completely online. An internet-based business is ideal for the entrepreneur who wants to sell but doesn't want the burden of maintaining a physical location or inventory. An online business also gives you the option of working from anywhere – all you need is a Wi-Fi connection!

Again, there is some overlap between this chapter and the others, as you can use the internet to sell products, services, entertainment, or your creative talents. If you already have a product or service but you like the idea of having an internet business, check back with those chapters for ideas of how they might be adapted to selling online.

1. Build a Halloween website

If you want to build an online business, creating a website is probably the first thing that comes to mind. It's certainly an essential part of establishing an online presence. Of course, if you want to make money from your site, you have to sell something – it could be a product, a service, or maybe advertising. You can also create a membership site with content that will have subscribers coming back to your page again and again and paying for the privilege.

Setting up a Halloween website is easier than you think! You can visit my website, Halloween-Lifestyle.com, to see how I did it… or just Google "Halloween website" and check out what other people are doing. There are hundreds of Halloween sites that you can get inspiration from.

To get your site up and running, you can hire a web designer. If you have the tech skills, you can design it yourself. Even if you don't, there are plenty of sites offering free or low-cost easy-to-use templates so practically anyone can create a good-looking website.

2. Sell products for others as an affiliate

This is a great alternative if you don't have a product of your own. Costumes are the biggest moneymaker for affiliate sales, but commissions are small. They vary between 5 and 15%, though you may find some lower or higher. The key is to figure out which niches will be the best this year and specialize. For example, everyone will sell zombie costumes, but few will offer specifically "plus-sized female zombie costumes."

You can also be an affiliate for Amazon or any site that offers such a program. Check out affiliate sites like cj.com and clickbank.com. There's a real science to being a successful affiliate, and a complete guide to affiliate income is beyond the scope of this book. However, there are many online courses and tutorials that will show you the ropes and teach you all about keywords, commissions, and setting up your site for success.

3. Write a Halloween blog

Write about general Halloween topics, decorating, ghost stories… anything that expresses your love of all things Halloween. Write short fiction. Make recommendations for costumes or décor or craft projects. By using good keywords and working through social media, you can grow your readership and start selling ads to monetize your blog. Again, you can visit my website, Halloween-Lifestyle.com, to get ideas for blog topics.

4. Sell instructions for do-it-yourselfers

You can make and sell step-by-step plans for individual projects or collect them into an EBook. If costume-making is your thing, you can offer downloadable sewing patterns. You might also consider selling all-included kits containing everything you need to do a particular project.

Halloween fans have an insatiable appetite for cool new Halloween projects. Need inspiration? Check out Pinterest or websites like www.instructables. com and www.marthastewart.com .

5. Start a YouTube channel

Produce your own videos demonstrating your skills at Halloween crafts, prop making, costuming, or makeup. You can monetize your channel with ads and also refer viewers back to your website where your products are for sale.

6. Develop an online learning course

Similar to what you might do on your YouTube channel, you can develop a tutorial for Udemy or other online learning site teaching the same skills.

7. Write an EBook

Online self-publishing is the way of the future! Your EBook doesn't have to be long. In fact, it might only be 20 pages or so. But that's okay! People like to buy short little EBooks to quickly download and read online or print out the parts they need, like recipes, instructions, or patterns. Of course, you would sell them at a low price point – sometimes just a few dollars or even less – but the more you can spread the word about your book, the more you'll sell. And the nice thing about self-publishing is that you get to keep all the money after the expenses are paid.

There are a number of internet outlets for self-publishing, and Kindle is the most popular online publisher. Amazon makes it super easy to self-publish and promote your book. They even have a print-on-demand program that allows you to sell print copies of your book without having to pay for an entire print run or maintain inventory.

You also have the option of setting up a sales page and selling your EBook from your own website.

Because I can only skim the surface in the confines of this book, I recommend you check out one of the many how-to books about EBook publishing and launch your career as an author!

8. Podcasting

Podcasts have been around for a while, but they're really just taking off in terms of their potential as a marketing tool or audience builder. A podcast is like internet radio, a program of music or talk available in digital format to be broadcasted and downloaded via the internet. You can listen on an iPod, your computer, your cell phone, or even in your car. Unlike radio, you can listen to a podcast whenever and wherever you want to, and you can subscribe to the ones you follow so you never miss new content.

Podcasting gives you the opportunity to become a home-based radio star with much greater reach than is possible with traditional radio. Anyone can record a show and broadcast it to people all over the world. The best part is that your listeners have access to your content at any time and place – while riding in the car, doing housework, eating in a restaurant, or even at work!

What kind of Halloween podcast can you produce? You can get ideas from the earlier chapters and do things like read scary stories in your best creepy voice, interview interesting people (perhaps other Halloween entrepreneurs?), talk about a spooky historical event, a visit to a haunt, or how to get a job at a Haunted Attraction…. The possibilities are limited only by your imagination!

CHAPTER 7

BRICKS AND MORTAR/YOUR PHYSICAL ASSETS

Your physical assets are any piece of tangible property that you own or have access to that can be used to make cash. So we're not just talking about bricks-and-mortar buildings, but any asset you own that you can rent to someone or that people can meet in, ride in, or party in, for example. Think barns, RVs, boats, hearses, cars, party tents, and so on.

Some folks are lucky enough to already own property, have access to a building, or own a suitable vehicle. If you don't, and this is your dream, it may require a bigger investment.

If you're lucky enough to own such assets or have access to them, here's my Top Ten list for Halloween businesses you can start:

1. Halloween Pop-Up Store

Temporary Halloween stores like Halloween Adventure and Spirit Halloween make a ton of money each year despite only having a retail location for about 3 months a year. You can emulate their success by getting a short-term lease on a vacant storefront from September 1st thru November 30th. You can extend your moneymaking season if your landlord will allow you to extend your lease for another couple months and turn it into a pop-up Christmas store!

2. Permanent Halloween Store

These are becoming more and more popular, as the Halloween Lifestyle takes over the world! Plenty of enterprising self-bossers are finding that there is a market for Halloween merchandise all year round. You could also turn this into your own global Halloween empire by opening a store online with your own website or through an Amazon or EBay store.

Whether you have a pop-up store or a permanent location, another idea would be to invite Halloween artists and crafters into your store to sell their work. Everybody wins – the artists have a place to sell, and you get a booth fee and a percentage of their sales.

3. Haunted Attraction

Opening your own haunted attraction is an expensive and extremely labor-intensive proposition, but it can be incredibly fun and rewarding. Before you invest in the time and money needed to open your own haunt, you must be VERY familiar with how this business works. In other words, you should have already worked in, designed, or help run a haunted house in the past. It also helps to surround yourself with people with the real world construction and design skills to make your facility top-notch.

You (or the people who work for you) should have business, PR, and marketing expertise, as well as design, fabrication, makeup, construction, and people skills. And of course, they should also have industry-specific knowledge.

Haunted attraction experts say the two hardest parts are getting a location and getting funding. Investigate the possibility of teaming up with a local facility like a family fun center, amusement park, water park or sports facility that isn't taking advantage of Halloween.

If you have access to an RV, why not turn it into a Haunted RV for the Halloween season? You can drive it around to locations to serve people at festivals like a food truck. Or you can park it in a set location and set up a graveyard/prop farm around it.

4. Party Room

If you have access to an indoor or outdoor space, you can throw your own Halloween parties during the month of October. A theme party is a bigger draw than a generic party – a murder mystery party is a popular choice for adults, while a mad scientist theme might appeal to kids.

For the price of admission, you can offer movies, food, or live entertainment. Don't be cheap – hire a caterer and give your guests their money's worth! This is another one of those opportunities where you can really profit from partnering with other businesses to keep costs down and provide more value for partygoers.

You can do the same with a barn or a picnic shelter. Or if your condo or apartment building has a party room, you may be able to use it. Charge $10 or more a head for admission to the party and give out wristbands so you know who's supposed to be there and who's not.

If you don't own or have unlimited access to a building, you can rent one. There are plenty of unused buildings that people would be happy to lease to you rather than let them sit idle.

5. Food truck

As I mentioned in the Haunted RV section, food trucks have become a pretty hot item lately. Basically, you buy or refurbish a truck and install a mini-kitchen. Then you can drive wherever you want and park the truck to sell your wares. Easy-to-carry foods are best. You can offer Halloween/fall-type foods like hot cider, donuts, or funnel cake, or even Halloween-themed foods like you'd serve at a party.

6 Hearse for Hire

Funeral homes eventually get rid of their old hearses in favor of a newer, shinier model. If you watched Six Feet Under on HBO, one of the characters inherited a used hearse and had it painted lime green. Think of the opportunities! You could trick out this vehicle and rent it for special occasions or even offer your services as a driver (wearing an undead chauffeur's costume, of course) for clients on Goth prom night or for a Halloween wedding or a cemetery tour.

7 Haunt-Themed Amusements

Think of the Monster Golf franchise or Laser Tag. It can be themed depending on whether your audience is children or adults.

8 Costume Shop/Rental

If you have use of a bricks-and-mortar location, why not keep your costume business (as described in Chapters 2 and 3) open all year long?

9 Themed Restaurant

This is what I referred to in Chapter 1 as a "Big Dream." The Jekyll and Hyde Club is a popular tourist spot in New York's Greenwich Village where guests are entertained by costumed wait- staff playing characters in a mad scientist's lab. It's a fabulous tourist trap, with Victorian décor, animatronic skeletons, thunder and lightning, and even a monster on a slab that descends from the ceiling. Obviously, this would require a big investment, but the payoff could be worth it.

10 Grow a pumpkin patch

If you have some land available that's not otherwise occupied, why not start your own pumpkin patch business?

You can make your pumpkin patch stand out by offering other attractions like a corn maze, spooky theater performances, hay rides, face painting, or a petting zoo. How about setting up a carving area where guests can carve their own jack-o-lanterns and not have to deal with the mess at home?

Remember that it takes a pumpkin about 4 months to grow, so it's important to start early in the year. If you want to keep selling all the way to Thanksgiving, plant a side crop of sugar (pie) pumpkins or colorful gourds or winter squash. After all your crops have been picked and the land cleared (broken or misshapen pumpkins and squash can be sold for livestock feed), your pumpkin patch can then be repurposed into a Christmas tree lot!

PARTING THOUGHTS

Thanks for sticking with me to the end! I've barely scratched the surface of potential Halloween entrepreneurship.

Because nobody thinks of everything, I'd love to hear about your moneymaking ideas. Email me at Maledicta@Halloween-Lifestyle.com.

Good luck in your business ventures...

And HAPPY HALLOWEEN!

Hauntingly,
Maledicta

Linda Johnson Tomsho, better known to the Halloween-Lifestyle Community as "Maledicta," is Mistress of the Dark and Proprietress of the Halloween-Lifestyle Empire (Halloween-Lifestyle.com and The Morbid Emporium).

She's a lifelong fanatic for all things Halloween. Horror, and Pop Culture whose philosophy is "Halloween isn't a holiday – it's a lifestyle!"

In the 90s, she co-founded the Edward D. Wood, Jr. Memorial Film Society, for which she hosts and coordinates monthly screenings of the best and worst of "Underappreciated Cinema" – horror, sci-fi, cult, or simply weird – and beyond. The Film Salon is still going strong after 25 years.

Linda is also the CIO (Chief Inspiration Officer) of Different Drummer Coaching, career coaching and start-up guidance for aspiring entrepreneurs with a flair for the strange and unusual... those who don't want to settle for something ordinary. Her mission is simple: To show people how to make money from doing what they love. Based on a "Life First, Work Second" philosophy, Linda helps clients realize what is possible for them and guides them through the process of launching their own Halloween or Horror-related businesses and/or lucrative side gigs.

Talk about practicing what you preach – When she's not engaged in her year-round Halloween business or screening weird cinema, she can often be found pursuing one of her side gigs as a freelance book coach, copywriter, or researcher.

Linda lives near Pittsburgh with her husband Matthew and Zelda, her faithful canine companion. She is the mother of three adult children, each following their own unique path in life. Linda has been active in dog rescue for over 20 years. Among her other passions are travel, history, music, and curating her eclectic collections.

Visit her website, Halloween-Lifestyle.com or Facebook page (Halloween Lifestyle Society) to join the Halloween-Lifestyle community.

If you'd like to find out how you can profit from your own passion for Halloween, drop her an email at Maledicta@Halloween-Lifestyle.com and sign up for a free 30-minute Discovery Session.

Made in the USA
Las Vegas, NV
25 June 2021